MAN
VERSUS
MOUNTAIN

MOUNT KILIMANJARO

Christine
Petersen

PURPLE TOAD
PUBLISHING

P.O. Box 631
Kennett Square, Pennsylvania 19348
www.purpletoadpublishing.com

K2 in Kashmir

Kilimanjaro

Mount Everest

Mount Fuji

Mount Olympus

Copyright © 2014 by Purple Toad Publishing, Inc.

Printing 1 2 3 4 5 6 7 8 9

PUBLISHER'S NOTE: The data in this book has been researched in depth, and to the best of our knowledge is factual. Although every measure is taken to give an accurate account, Purple Toad Publishing makes no warranty of the accuracy of the information and is not liable for damages caused by inaccuracies.

Note: Purple Toad Publishing is not advocatiing mountain climbing for children and will not assume any liability for damages.

Publisher's
Cataloging-in-Publication Data

Petersen, Christine
   Mount Kilimanjaro / Christine Petersen
   p. cm.—(Man versus mountain)
   Includes bibliographic references and index.
      ISBN: 978-1-62469-058-7 (library bound)
   1. Kilimanjaro, Mount (Tanzania)—Juvenile literature.   I. Title.
                              DT449.K4 2013
                              916.7826—dc23
                                 2013936510

eISBN: 9781624690594

Printed by Lake Book Manufacturing, Chicago, IL

CONTENTS

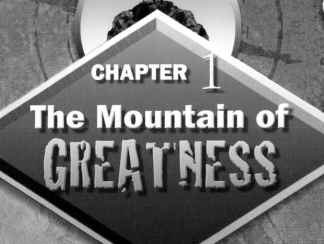

The Mountain of GREATNESS

Johannes Rebmann never planned to become an explorer. When the young German arrived on the coast of East Africa in 1846, he was totally focused on his work as a missionary.[1] Rebmann spent his life teaching native Africans about Christianity.

His home base was Mombasa, a bustling city on the Indian Ocean. Missionary work took Rebmann to villages dotting the nearby countryside. Before long, he was traveling far inland. This part of Africa was unfamiliar to missionaries. Few Europeans had been there at all. His travels led to the foot of Africa's tallest mountain, Kilimanjaro. He would introduce the world to this spectacular place—even if they refused to believe what he wrote.

No Ordinary Mountain

A few months after Rebmann arrived in Mombasa, an African man arrived at his church. He would help to

Kilimanjaro is surrounded by a savanna, a tree-dotted grassland that supports large herds of elephants and other grazing animals.

Johannes Rebmann

translate the Bible from English to Swahili, the most common local language. The man talked as they worked. Rebmann especially liked his story about an immense mountain that was located far west of Mombasa. It was called Kilimanjaro, Swahili for "the mountain of greatness."

The mountain was an important landmark, for it could be seen from a great distance. Travelers from Mombasa used Kilimanjaro to point the way west. Traders from inland kingdoms rode past it on the way to markets along the coast. Everyone stopped to collect water from streams that rushed off its steep, forested slopes.

At this point in the story, the man's voice dropped to a whisper. This was no ordinary mountain, he told Rebmann. Kilimanjaro was the home of jinn—evil spirits who punished anyone who entered their realm. The man's son had been to Kilimanjaro. He saw a group of travelers after they tried to climb the mountain. "The powder of the guns did not go off," the son had reported; "the legs and other parts of the body became stiff, and many people died of the bad effects of the jinn."[2] You might ask why anyone would climb a mountain if they believed it to be inhabited by evil spirits. The storyteller explained this, too. Atop the mountain was a substance that glimmered and shone like silver.

Rebmann did not believe in jinn, but he was curious. He would have to see this mountain for himself.

In the Distance

In 1848, Rebmann made plans for a long trip inland. He hoped to befriend chiefs of the Chagga tribe and convert them to Christianity.

These people lived and farmed on the southern slopes of Kilimanjaro. From their villages, he could see the mountain up close.

The first challenge was simply to reach Kilimanjaro. Between the coast and the mountain lay a vast expanse of savanna. Rebmann's trusted African guide found a path through this tree-dotted grassland. They passed herds of elephants, rhinos, zebras, antelopes, and giraffes moving across the plains from one watering hole to the next. Powerful predators were never far behind. Rebmann's party was on constant watch for leopards and hyenas. African lions were another concern. Traveling in large family groups, or prides, lions ruled the savanna. A male lion was regal and handsome in his mane of fur. But he might weigh 415 pounds (189 kilograms)—more than twice as much as a man.[3] Smaller females were skilled hunters able to catch even fast-running gazelles. Lions rarely hunted humans, but it was best to be careful in their territory. By May 11, the group had been traveling for

African lions are among the most powerful predators living in the grasslands near Kilimanjaro. Historically, lions sometimes wandered up the mountain slopes.

almost two weeks. That morning, Rebmann climbed to the top of a hill to look around. There it was! A massive, cone-shaped mountain seemed to fill the western horizon. Just as he had heard, its summit sparkled in the sunlight.

Rebmann turned to his guide. He was about to ask whether this brightness looked like a cloud on the mountaintop. Then he stopped and smiled knowingly. Of course! Like mountains he had seen in Europe, Kilimanjaro wore a cap of snow atop its highest peak.

Rebmann made three visits to Kilimanjaro, but he never tried to climb "the mountain of greatness." A man of the people, he stayed below in the Chagga villages. Still, he understood that it was important to describe Kilimanjaro for geographers back in Europe who had never been there. Rebmann hiked through the hilly, forested countryside of Chagga territory. He spent hours gazing up at the mountain. Up close, it became obvious that Kilimanjaro had two high summits. One was slightly lower with a jagged top, while the other was a tall dome. The Chagga had names for both peaks. The lower was Mawenzi (mah-WHEN-zee) and the higher was Kibo (KEE-bow). Rebmann learned that kibo means "snow" in the Chagga language.[4] A third peak called Shira (SHEER-uh) was identified decades later. Shira's summit had been worn down over time, so Rebmann could have mistaken it for a flat slope on the northwest side of Mawenzi.

He now understood why travelers believed that evil spirits lived on Kilimanjaro. Most Africans were used to warm weather. They would not recognize snow. Visitors might climb the mountain thinking they saw silver atop it. Instead, they would find freezing temperatures and ice. It was natural for them to blame evil spirits for something so unfamiliar. The Chagga did not have to fear jinn on their mountain. They saw snow fall on Kilimanjaro every year and understood that snow melts into water.

Rebmann noticed that Kilimanjaro changed from season to season. The mountain is only about 200 miles (320 kilometers) south of the equator. Regions near the equator are described as the tropics. Tropical environments do not have the four seasons (Spring, Summer, Fall, and Winter) familiar to people in many other parts of the world. Instead, there are wet and dry seasons. Around Kilimanjaro, the wettest months are November and December. Mild rains come again in April and May. The times in between are dry. Rebmann wrote that Mawenzi was "richly and very far down covered with snow"[5] during the rains. This melted in dry months, leaving Mawenzi bare. Tall Kibo always had a snowy cap. During the rainy season, the snow reached farther down the slope.

No Snow?

In 1849, Rebmann wrote an article for his church's magazine. His goal was to share knowledge of the Chagga people and their homeland. The story included information about the great mountain of Kilimanjaro.

At the time, English geographer William Desborough Cooley of England was considered the world's expert on Africa. He was drawing a

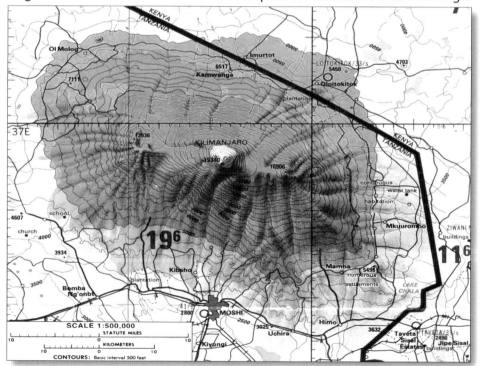

This topographic map shows Kilimanjaro's increasing elevation, or height.

detailed map of the continent—even though he had never traveled there. Cooley laughed at Rebmann's description of Kilimanjaro. Snow could not possibly form near the equator, where it is always hot! "I deny altogether the existence of snow on Mount Kilimanjaro," Cooley stated.[6] No one wanted to disagree with this powerful man, and Kilimanjaro was ignored. Instead, European explorers investigated other parts of Africa and the world.

More than a decade later, naturalist Claus Carl von der Decken became curious about Kilimanjaro. In 1861 and 1863, he attempted to climb the mountain. Although he never reached the top, he made important observations along the way. He noted that Kilimanjaro is made of lava rocks. Lava comes from Earth's mantle, the layer that lies under its hard surface. Gooey, hot lava is released during volcanic eruptions. It hardens when it cools. Even millions of years later, these

Huge chunks of rock scattered across the high slopes of Kilimanjaro are a reminder of the mountain's fiery volcanic origins.

volcanic rocks are easy to recognize. Lava rocks proved to Von der Decken that Kilimanjaro is a volcanic mountain. He also estimated Kilimanjaro's elevation. Von der Decken said that Kibo rose to about 20,000 feet (6,100 meters) above sea level—which is close to today's measured elevation.

The last issue was snow. One night while Von der Decken and his team were camped on the mountain, fresh snow fell on their tents. He wrote about it, and Cooley read the account. Cooley still refused to believe.

Charles New provided the final evidence in 1871. With his African companion Tofiki, New climbed Kilimanjaro up to its snowline. This is the elevation above which snow is always present. New and Tokifi found a deep layer of snow on Kilimanjaro. They were unable to climb past it. Geographers then had to admit that snow could fall atop high mountains—even in the tropics.

German climbers Hans Meyer and Ludwig Purtscheller were the first Europeans to reach the summit of Kilimanjaro. They stood atop Kibo on October 6, 1889. It is possible that they were the first people ever to reach that high, windy peak.

Hans Meyer

Wanderer Above the Sea of Fog, painted in 1818, portrays a romantic view of mountain climbing from the European perspective of the time.

Reaching the Summit

African people have lived around Kilimanjaro for thousands of years. As hunters and farmers, they spent a lot of time exploring the lower slopes. Local people also crossed the high pass between Mawenzi and Kibo to trade or fight with tribes on the other side. But they may not have had any reason to try climbing the snowy summit. Europeans had a different attitude. In the mid-nineteenth century, climbing mountains became a fascination. Climbers were eager to conquer high peaks worldwide. Mountain climbing became more than a way to learn the geography of new places. It was a pastime for the wealthy and a way for people to test their skills in the most challenging situations. People have been climbing mountains for sport ever since.

Kilimanjaro grows more popular every year. Kili, as it is now fondly known, is the tallest mountain in Africa. It is taller than the highest mountains on three other continents as well. Stack thirteen Empire State Buildings atop each other and they still won't match the height of this mountain. Despite its soaring height, no fancy climbing gear or experience is required to reach the top. In an average year, more than 35,000 people try it.[7] About half make it.[8] What does it take to reach the top? "Pole, pole," the guides will tell you in Swahili. "Slowly, slowly."

Scientists have made fascinating discoveries about how Kilimanjaro was formed. Far below East Africa, two massive bubbles of magma rose from the mantle. They pushed against the continent's rocky surface, slowly lifting the land upward. That's why much of East Africa is high above sea level. The rigid continental rock has cracked from all the pressure. This crack is called the Great Rift Valley. It begins near Africa's east coast in Mozambique and extends about 4,000 miles (6,400 kilometers) northeast toward Syria.

Pressure from the magma bubbles was released in volcanic eruptions. Less than a million years ago, one of these Great Rift Valley eruptions formed Shira. A later blast produced Mawenzi. Finally, just 360,000 years ago, Kibo erupted between them. For a volcano, Kilimanjaro is young.

Over time, water and wind have eroded Shira's cone. Mawenzi's broken top also shows its age. Neither of these volcanoes will erupt again. Kibo's last major eruption was thousands of years ago, but its bubbling heart remains active. Inside the bowl-shaped crater, vents continue to release volcanic gases and ash. The ground is hot to touch. Along Kibo's southeast slope are about 250 mini-volcanoes. Through these, Kibo lets off steam between major eruptions.

Like Shira and Mawenzi, Kibo is beginning to erode. Its highest point stands 19,341 feet (5,895 meters) above sea level. Will the mountain erupt again before Kibo becomes flat like Shira? Some scientists think it's just a matter of time.

Kili is not the only glacier-topped mountain in Africa. Not far from Kilimanjaro, in the neighboring country of Kenya, is Mount Kenya. At 17,052 feet (5,199 meters) tall, this dormant volcanic mountain is also popular with climbers. The local people, including the Kikuyu, Embu, Ameru, and Maasai, are farmers who depend on Mount Kenya's snowmelt for water.

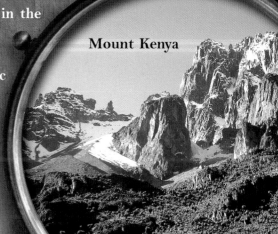

Mount Kenya

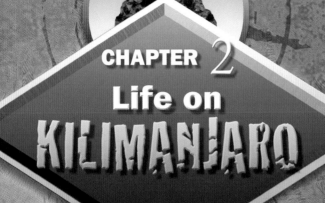

CHAPTER 2
Life on
KILIMANJARO

Kilimanjaro is located in Tanzania, a nation on the eastern coast of Africa. Tanzania is home to about 47 million people.[1] Of these, 1.5 million live within sight of the great mountain.[2]

Humans have probably always lived near Kilimanjaro. Ancient carved stone bowls and knife blades have been found around its base. Some of these are almost 3,000 years old. People in this region learned to make iron about 2,000 years ago. Iron is a strong metal used for forging tools, weapons, and ornaments. For the past 300 years, Kilimanjaro has been home to the Chagga people. They are skilled farmers who grow food crops in the rich volcanic soil. Their neighbors are the Maasai, a proud group of people who live on the wide, grassy savanna surrounding the mountain. Over the centuries, many Maasai have preserved their traditional way of life as cattle herders.

Chagga home gardens, or *kihambas*, are almost as lush as the wild rainforest itself.

Traditionally, Chagga people lived in rounded huts near their kihambas. Woven from banana leaves and other natural materials, the huts stayed cool during the summer months.

Home Gardens

On a map, the Chagga homeland looks like a wide band across the southern base of the mountain. This is called "the cultivated zone" because most of the land has been farmed. Over time, Chagga land has been divided into small *kihambas,* or home gardens.[3] These gardens are passed from one generation to the next. Kihambas are not like the farms that grow rows of plants in an open field. In kihambas, tall trees, medium-sized shrubs, and ground-hugging crops are all grown together. In this way, one family can grow dozens of plants in a very small space.

Chagga farmers live right next to Kilimanjaro's rainforest. Rainforest trees are often left to grow on the kihambas. They provide fruit, medicines, and firewood. These big trees are also an important source of shade in the dry season. Their roots hold water and soil in the ground.

Bananas are the most important food in the Chagga diet. About fifteen kinds of bananas are planted on the kihambas. Each has a unique look and taste. No part of the banana goes to waste. After the fruit is eaten, leaves and peels are fed to goats and other livestock on the farm. Coffee is grown alongside bananas in the middle levels of the kihamba. The Chagga harvest coffee beans to sell worldwide.

Vegetables grow on the ground below all these other plants. Bean and pea vines snake up nearby trees. Cassava is a root that looks like a yam. Sorghum, millet, and rice grains can be cooked in many ways or fed to livestock.

Rain and Snow

On the savanna of eastern Africa, 20 to 60 inches (50 to 150 centimeters) of rain falls each year. Most of it pours down during the rainy season, with only about 4 inches (10 centimeters) falling during the long, dry season. But on Kilimanjaro, more than 90 inches (230 centimeters) of rain may fall each year. How does Kilimanjaro get so much more rain than the area around it?

Rain comes to Kilimanjaro from two main sources: evaporation from the grasslands, rainforest, and snowmelt, and from seasonal winds that blow off the Indian Ocean. Evaporation is the change of water from liquid to vapor. Water used by plants is released in the form of vapor. Warm air rising off the grasslands carries water vapor. When these air currents reach the mountainside, they are forced upward. At higher altitudes, the air becomes cool. Water in the air gathers together, forming clouds. It falls again as rain or snow.

On Kilimanjaro, the rainforest plants release even more water vapor into the air. Melting snow and rainwater seep into soils and run down the hillside into streams. Water evaporates from these sources as well. With this steady supply of water vapor, clouds form over the mountain almost every day. Between March and May, winds blow off the Indian Ocean, bringing moisture-laden clouds inland to deposit yet more rain on the slopes of Kilimanjaro.

Even in summer, Kilimanjaro's highest summit at Uhuru Peak often carries a blanket of snow and ice that makes climbing a challenge.

Long ago, the Chagga learned to use Kilimanjaro's water cycle to provide a steady supply of water for their kihambas. They dug a complex system of canals leading away from local streams. This irrigation system was so important that the whole village helped to manage it. People took turns cleaning the canals. They worked together to repair any damage. And everyone took equal shares of water.

Modern Chagga villages still have canal systems. They may also have pipes. But it is not always easy to get water. In recent years, Kilimanjaro has not had as much rain. Its streams do not run as full as they once did. Experts think that lack of water is connected to the size of Kilimanjaro's forest.

Satellite pictures show that large blocks of rainforest around Kili have been cut down.[4] Logging companies take some of the wood. They sell it for building material. Local people play a role, too. Above the rainforest lies a region called "the heath zone." It is home to giant heather plants that are often cut and burned to make charcoal. (Charcoal is an inexpensive fuel used for heat and cooking.)

Since 1973 the mountain has been a national park, so it is illegal to cut down trees on Kilimanjaro. Why would people break the law? Logging companies can make a lot of money from selling wood from trees. It is hard for rangers to catch them all in the huge park. Local people cut trees because they are hungry, cold, or need money. Tanzania is one of the poorest nations in the world. The Chagga are hardworking people, but there is not enough land to support everyone.

Cutting the forest solves people's needs for a while, but it causes more problems in the long run. Usually Kilimanjaro's forests absorb water that is delivered during rainstorms. The trees produce more clouds through evaporation. As the forest grows smaller, this process breaks down. Rain doesn't fall on the gardens and people can't get enough water for irrigation. To survive, they are forced to cut more of the forest or leave the mountain.

Furtwängler is one of only sixteen glaciers remaining on Kibo.

Lack of water also affects the glaciers on Kilimanjaro. Glaciers form when snow falls and does not melt over long periods of time. These rivers of ice are common at Earth's poles and on mountain slopes. The heavy ice moves slowly downhill, scraping over everything in its path. When Meyer and Purtscheller climbed Kilimanjaro in 1889, Kibo was covered in ice.[5] Glaciers overflowed from its crater like frozen fingers reaching down the mountainside. The glaciers no longer form a solid cap over the crater. Instead, the ice is broken into three sections with large areas of bare rock in between. By 2012, only sixteen glaciers could be found on Kibo. This is less than one-fifth the amount of ice that was there just a century ago.[6]

In 2000, researchers drilled into a glacier near Kibo's rim. They took a sample of ice from the very bottom. They knew this would be the oldest ice in the glacier. How long had it been there? Tests showed that the ice was about 9,000 years old.[7] If the ice continues to disappear at its current pace, Kilimanjaro's ancient glaciers will be gone within a few decades.

Some scientists are concerned that Kili's glaciers are disappearing because of climate change. Climate change occurs when carbon dioxide and certain other chemicals build up in the atmosphere. These chemicals can cause the atmosphere to become thinner in some places. They can also trap heat that would normally escape into space. The planet grows steadily warmer and weather patterns change. Climate change has affected glaciers around the world, including Kilimanjaro's glaciers. But can you guess another reason why Kili's glaciers are melting? It is due to the loss of trees.

Clouds and trees work together to cool the dark volcanic rocks and soil. Without them, temperatures around Kili have increased. Local people speak with surprise of not needing sweaters at night. They complain of heat during the day.

When clouds don't form, Kilimanjaro's glaciers sit in direct sunshine. At this elevation, the sun is powerful and bright. Ice becomes slushy if the temperature rises close to 32°F (0°C). Even when temperatures stay

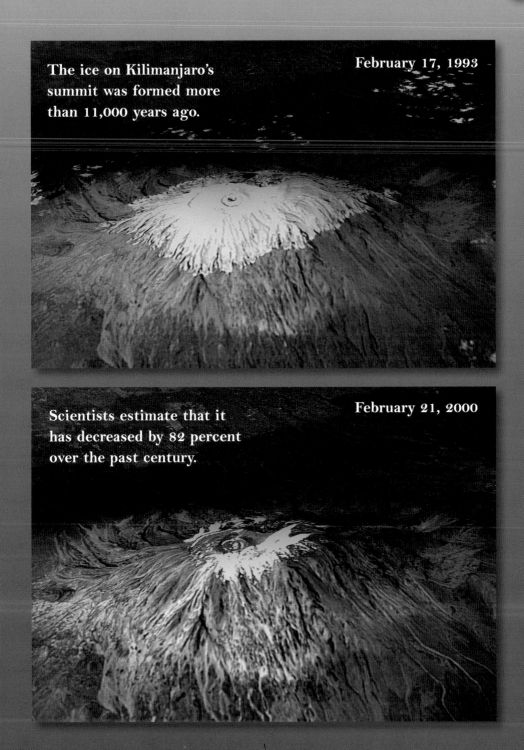

The ice on Kilimanjaro's summit was formed more than 11,000 years ago.

February 17, 1993

Scientists estimate that it has decreased by 82 percent over the past century.

February 21, 2000

Tanzanian people are working to protect their environment. One effort is the Keep Kili Clean initiative, in which mountain porters and guides clean up trash and plant trees.

below freezing, the ice sublimates and water vapor rises into the dry air. There is no longer as much snowfall during the rainy season, either. The ice is disappearing faster than it can be replaced.[8]

Planting for the Future

On the lower slopes of Mount Kilimanjaro sits the town of Moshi. The townspeople there have decided to make a difference in their community by planting trees. In 2012, they hoped to plant 1,680,000 of them.[9]

Years ago, people planted trees such as eucalyptus and Mexican pine at Kilimanjaro. Those trees are not native to Africa but were brought in from other continents. Some species were brought for the production of lumber. They were not meant to be left in place for hundreds of years. They cannot be part of a healthy African forest. Eucalyptus burns easily, and both species spread into places where native trees used to grow. The people of Moshi chose to plant fruit trees such as mango, orange, and avocado. Once in the ground, these trees will provide food for people and wildlife. They will help to restore the water cycle and they will bring hope of a healthier future.

Archaeologists study human history and culture. Louis and Mary Leakey were pioneers in this field of science. One of their most exciting fossils came from Oldupai Gorge. Located barely 60 miles (100 kilometers) from Kilimanjaro, Oldupai is a steep-sided canyon inside an old volcano.

Rocks form in layers there, one atop the other. Older rocks are on the bottom and newer ones are on the top. That clue helps archaeologists figure out the age of rocks in a particular place. As rocks form, anything on the surface will be trapped within their layers. Heat and pressure during this process cause some objects to crumble. Others harden into fossils.

The Leakeys hoped to find hominid fossils that could explain human evolution. The hominid group of animals includes humans and their ancient relatives. At Oldupai in 1959, Mary unearthed a small, broken skull. Based on its location, she figured that this hominid had lived 1.75 million years ago. It would have stood about 4 feet (1.4 meters) tall and had a huge jaw with strong teeth. Scientists call it *Paranthropus*, or "Almost Man."[10]

In 1976, another remarkable fossil was found west of Oldupai. Archaeologists explored a layer of rock that formed from volcanic ash about 3.6 million years ago. In this layer they saw a long line of hominid footprints. These prove that even our most ancient ancestors walked on two legs. They lived in East Africa long before Kilimanjaro was there.

Paranthropus on Plains
by Walter Voigt

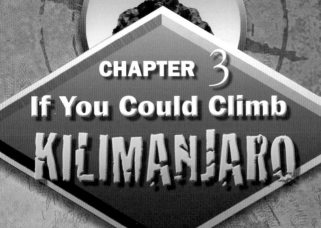

CHAPTER 3
If You Could Climb
KILIMANJARO

Climbing Kilimanjaro is much more than a vacation adventure. It is a serious physical challenge. Imagine you are planning a trip to the summit of Kilimanjaro. How would you prepare?

The first step would be to get a passport. This small booklet is issued by your national government and proves that you are traveling legally. Every traveler must show a passport when entering a new country.

Knowing the health risks in other countries is vital for travel. Travelers to Kilimanjaro typically visit a doctor several weeks before going to Tanzania. Besides making sure your regular vaccines are up to date, he or she will recommend additional vaccines to prevent diseases that are uncommon where you live but troublesome in Tanzania. Malaria is not a problem on Kilimanjaro. The mountain is too high and cold for mosquitoes that carry this disease. However, if you are planning a trip to the savanna, the doctor will probably add anti-malarial drugs to your list.

Kibo is such a high summit that it rises
above the cloud layer.

You must be in good health to reach the summit of Kilimanjaro. The key is endurance rather than super-strength. (Endurance is the ability to exercise for long periods of time.) A typical Kilimanjaro trek covers about 40 miles (64 kilometers) in 5 to 8 days.[1] Most of the climb is uphill on muddy, rocky, or snowy trails. All of the walking takes place at high altitude. That makes it hard to get enough oxygen. The best preparation is walking over increasing distances and in different conditions. Strong lungs, legs, and back muscles will improve endurance. You must be able to walk at a slow but steady pace for up to eight hours on Kilimanjaro.

There are seven trails to choose from. Five of these go up the mountain. One comes down. The seventh trail goes both ways. There is also a loop trail, which begins partway up the mountain and circles the base of Kibo. Most treks start at Marangu or Moshi, towns on the south side of the mountain. A few trekkers choose routes that begin from Arusha to the southwest. One trail begins on the opposite side of Kili, at Loitokitok in Kenya.

Everyone must hire a guide to trek in Kilimanjaro National Park. Guides have specific responsibilities. They provide food and cook meals

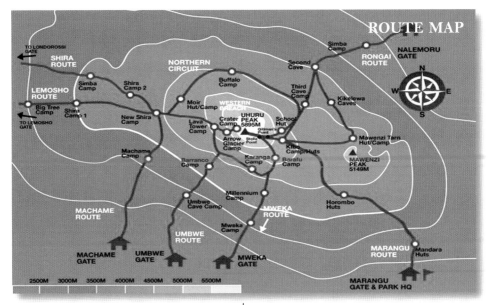

ROUTE MAP

on the trail. Guides also provide camping gear. They hire porters who carry everything up the mountain—including your bags. While the trekkers are trudging up the trail every afternoon, porters are already at camp setting up tents and preparing dinner.

People climb Kilimanjaro in all seasons of the year, but it is safest to do so during the dry season. That includes the months of February through March and July through September. Trekking during the rainy season is less crowded, but it adds dangerous challenges to an already difficult climb.

What to Pack?

Weather on Kilimanjaro can change quickly. Rainstorms are ever-present in the forest. Mist hangs over the heath zone. The sun can fry your skin near the summit, or wind can chap it. And no matter how hot it gets during the day, the nights often turn cold. The solution to all of these problems is careful packing. Here are a few tips:

- Most experts recommend wearing layers. Air is trapped between each item of clothing. It warms up from your body heat. Add or remove layers to adjust your temperature.
- Instead of t-shirts, bring a couple of light-weight, long-sleeved shirts made of wicking materials and two or three fleece pullovers.
- Leave jeans at home. Buy convertible outdoor pants with zip-off legs. You can make them into shorts when it's warm.
- Socks can take up a lot of space. Pack only two pairs each of thick and thin socks.
- Buy sturdy waterproof boots. Break them in beforehand to reduce the risk of blisters.
- Pack a billed cap and another hat made of fleece or wool. Add a pair of thick gloves. Keeping your head and hands warm can make the difference between misery and comfort on this mountain.
- Don't forget sunglasses.

- Only carry essential personal items: soap, a comb or brush, deodorant, a washcloth and towel, and plenty of toilet paper.
- A first-aid kit should hold bandages, moleskin for blisters, and antibiotic ointment. Pack over-the-counter pain relievers, and don't forget sunscreen and lip balm.
- Drink, drink, drink while hiking! Keep an insulated water bottle close at all times, and refill at each day's campsite.
- Trekking guides will provide most camping supplies, but you must bring a sleeping bag. Make sure it is lightweight but designed to keep you warm in below-freezing temperatures.

Experienced trekkers find ways to keep it simple, fitting all of their belongings into two bags. Pack almost everything into a large, sturdy backpack or duffel bag. Zip food, cameras, books, and wet clothes into separate plastic bags. Also, choose a daypack that is small and comfortable. It's smart to bring a big rain poncho that will fit over you and your daypack.

Tourists have a big impact on Kilimanjaro. Know the rules before you hike or camp anywhere. At Kilimanjaro, the park requires that you:

- Stay on trails rather than slide down slopes.
- Don't use fire anywhere on the mountain.
- Make sure every scrap of trash is disposed of properly—including toilet paper.

It's not easy to plan a trip like this. But it's worth the effort. Kilimanjaro offers dozens of wonders for every challenge.

Hans Meyer and Ludwig Purtscheller became famous after reaching the summit of Kilimanjaro. However, they could not have done it alone.

Meyer knew he needed the blessing of a Chagga chief to climb the mountain. The chief of Marangu gave his approval. He even helped Meyer and Purtscheller find five or six young men to hire as porters and guides.

Chagga guides were usually hunters who knew the best paths through the thick forest. They were familiar with the mountain's plants, wildlife, and weather. Porters were essential, too. These men did most of the heavy work—carrying equipment up the slope, setting up camp, and cooking.

In 1889, glaciers covered much of Kibo's summit. Other climbers had failed because they couldn't get across the ice. Meyer planned to set up camps at several points of elevation along the route. The key to success was food. The porters would bring up fresh supplies every few days. As history shows, Meyer's plan worked.

One hundred years later, the government of Tanzania chose to honor the African men who helped Meyer succeed. One of them was still living in Marangu, a town at the foot of the mountain. Yohani Kinyala Lauwo was just a teenager when he joined Meyer's team in 1889. He told interviewers that he made the trip wearing no shoes. Lauwo went on to become a guide, leading many trips up Kilimanjaro. He died in 1996, having lived about 125 years.[2]

A Chagga guide

CHAPTER 4
On the
TRAIL

Climbing Kilimanjaro provides a glimpse of an entirely different world. Treks begin from Moshi and other towns in the Chagga cultivated area. In just a short time, trekkers pass through six or seven ecosystems. (An ecosystem is a group of plants and animals suited to live in a particular environment.) Some people compare it to climbing through the seasons—from summer to winter in less than a week.

Many trekkers agree that the Machame Route is the prettiest trail on Kilimanjaro. It begins at the lower edge of Kili's rainforest, about 50 miles (80 kilometers) from Moshi. Groups gather under the gate's pointed roof early on the first morning. Everyone signs the ranger's book. They adjust backpacks and glance up the trail, feeling both nervous and eager. If they are lucky, in six days they will stand atop Uhuru Peak, the highest point on Kibo. Only two additional days are needed to hike straight back down the mountain along the Mweka Route.

What a thrill it must be to reach the top!

CONGRATULATIONS
YOU ARE NOW AT
UHURU PEAK, TANZANIA 5895M. AMSL.
AFRICA'S HIGHEST POINT
WORLD'S HIGHEST FREE-STANDING MOUNTAIN.
ONE OF WORLD'S LARGEST VOLCANOES.
WELCOME

The Machame Route is not the shortest way up Kilimanjaro. Nor is it the easiest. Most of the other routes can be completed in about 6 or 7 days. So why do more people reach the summit using Machame? An extra day on the mountain helps trekkers adjust to the altitude. That reduces the risk of altitude sickness.

In the Rainforest

The Machame Route passes through all of Kilimanjaro's ecosystems. It begins near the rainforest zone at an elevation of 5,942 feet (1,811 meters). There, huge fig and holly trees grow so tall and close that they block out the sun. Greenish-gray lichens hang from the trees like living streamers. On the forest floor, brilliant wildflowers grow. Some of these species are found only on the slopes of Kilimanjaro. One familiar plant is the delicate, purple-flowered African violet. Decades ago collectors took samples of African violets from the mountain. These plants are now sold around the world.

Moss plays an important role in this soggy environment. Like sponges, mosses absorb water and let it seep into the soil. Additional water runs across the ground. Trickles gather into streams that flow rapidly downhill. During the afternoon rain showers, the trail can get slippery with mud. Walk carefully, keeping an eye out for branches and rocks in the way.

When you feel tired, look up at the forest around you. Droplets of water hang from fern fronds, catching the sunlight like crystals. Brightly-patterned butterflies hover under large leaves. Ants march in straight lines across the path. Larger animals tend to hide, but their voices echo through the trees. Black and white colobus monkeys leap through the treetops in search of ripe fruit, or perch to watch you pass. They look dressed for a party in sleek black fur with flowing white strands down their backs. At night, you might hear the devilish shriek of a tree hyrax. A high-pitched whistle means that a bush baby is nearby. These tiny mammals are almost too cute to be real, with jaunty ears, huge eyes, and long back legs for jumping. Birds are easier to locate as they flit

Black-and-white colobus monkeys are among many spectacular animals that live in the rainforests at the foot of Kilimanjaro.

past, voicing sweet songs. The speckled mousebird lives in Kili's rainforest. A plain brown creature, it has a long, sweeping tail and a tall crest on its head.

Most hikers reach the edge of the rainforest by late afternoon. At 9,200 feet (2,800 meters), the heath zone begins. Because these plants are not as tall, the campsite will have a clear view of Kibo high overhead.

In the Middle

The second day on the Machame Route leads onto Shira. Its landscape is scattered with dark, volcanic rocks. In the morning you'll scrabble over some larger rock piles on the trail. These were either tossed off when Kibo erupted or they tumbled down later from the slopes above.

The heath zone is often wrapped in clouds, but it doesn't get heavy rainfall. Most precipitation there comes from mist. Plants in the heath zone must use less water than elsewhere on Kili. Grasses have deep roots that can find water underground. Heather bushes solve the problem by growing many small leaves that can collect mist. The sugarbush plant takes yet another approach. Its leaves have a tough outer layer to hold water inside the plant.

The heath zone is not lush and green like the rainforest, yet it has its own beauty. Wild irises and orchids grow along the trail. Red-hot pokers are native only to Africa. These tubular flowers grow in flame-colored clusters on tall stalks. White-necked ravens are common on this part of the trail. These large, black birds scoop up scraps of food that people leave behind. Four-striped grass mice have the same idea. They are frequent visitors to campsites. Elephants, giraffes, and African buffaloes once roamed this far up the mountainside in search of food or water. They are rare today. But trekkers sometimes report seeing eland. These spiral-horned antelope graze on grasses and leaves in the heath zone, and are well camouflaged against the earth-colored landscape.

The campsite on Shira is on the wide-open moorland. This ecosystem is rocky and dry. Temperatures may still be warm during the day but usually drop below freezing at night. To deal with these extremes, most moorland plants grow low to the ground. Rocks hold heat that plants can share. The landscape may feel windy and lonesome. This is a good time to bundle up and visit with porters and fellow climbers. On clear nights, stars spread out overhead like a river.

The third campsite on the Machame Route is at Lava Tower. At an elevation of 15,000 feet (4,572 meters), this spot is almost as high as the tallest mountains of Antarctica and Oceania. Some people climb the 200-foot (61-meter) Lava Tower for great views of the mountain and clouds below. Up there you can really feel the effects of the altitude. Appetite loss and headaches are common. Guides suggest eating small

The Western Breach is a steep slope near the summit of Kibo that is prone to rockslides.

amounts of food, taking headache medicine if necessary, and getting as much sleep as possible.

At the Top

In the past, experienced climbers would leave the main trail at Lava Tower. They would take a shortcut across a steep rock wall called the Western Breach. But the glacier there is rapidly shrinking, leaving loose rocks that tumble down without warning. In 2006, a rockslide in this area killed three American climbers. Many guides and porters in their group were badly injured. The Western Breach trail was closed for a while. Even when it's open, experts advise to avoid it completely.[1]

The route from Lava Tower is not life-threatening, but it has a few challenges. On this section of the trail, both hands are needed to

Giant groundsels are common in Kilimajaro's Great Barranco Valley. These odd-looking plants are adapted for dry, cold mountainous environments.

scramble up the high Barranco Wall. This tumble of rocks formed thousands of years ago from a massive landslide. Watch your footing on the other side. The trail crosses loose gravel as it dips into a lovely moorland valley.

It seems backward to go downslope when climbing a mountain, but this is a worthwhile detour for two reasons. First, it gives trekkers time to adjust to the altitude. Second, the trail leads into the Great Barranco Valley. Although it is in the moorland zone, plants there look as if they belong in a desert oasis. Giant groundsels can reach a height of 16 feet (5 meters). Their leaves grow in tight spirals, one layer surrounding another like a head of lettuce. When the outside layer dies, it wraps around the trunk to protect the tree from the cold.[2] Lobelia plants are short, but have a similar crown of leaves. Both plants open

A lammergeier

during the day and close at night to prevent freezing. Malachite sunbirds with shimmering green feathers thrive here. They probe with long beaks inside lobelia flowers to find insects.

After camping in a nearby valley, the fifth day's route follows the side of the mountain. It's a fairly easy walk to Barafu camp, which has good views of Kilimanjaro's southern glaciers. Their faces are sculpted into ridges and waves. This is the alpine desert zone, where less than 8 inches (20 centimeters) of rain falls per year. The alpine desert can be very windy. Sunlight reflects off bare rocks, bringing some daytime temperatures to a broiling 100°F (38°C). At sunset, temperatures plummet below freezing.

Despite the harsh conditions, living things find a way to survive there. Trekkers sometimes see lammergeiers soaring on wind currents at this altitude. These elegant-looking vultures are the cleanup crew, eating other animals that die on the high slopes. Lichens and mosses spread across the rocks. A hardy group of plants called "everlastings" can be found there, too. Their rainbow-colored blossoms grow in scattered mounds across the landscape.

Very little can live in the arctic summit zone above 16,500 feet (5,000 meters). Some everlastings have been found inside Kilimanjaro's crater, near vents that release volcanic gases. And once in a while climbers see the bodies of large animals high on the slopes of Kilimanjaro. Elephant bones were once found near the rocky summit of Mawenzi, at 16,000 feet (4,877 meters).[3] In the 1920s, trekkers saw a frozen leopard on Kibo. It had climbed almost to the summit. That spot is still known as Leopard Point. What brings these creatures to such a high place? Perhaps it is simply the search for food. Then again, maybe humans aren't the only ones curious enough to find out what it's like to stand at the top of the world.

Trekkers are awakened in the middle of the night to reach the summit. They sleepily put on all their layers of clothing and strap on headlights to find their way in the darkness. It's a slow, hard climb. Some people feel this is the hardest thing they've ever done. How do they make it? They go one step at a time, breath by breath. From the summit, it seems possible to see all of Africa spread out below.

Johannes Rebmann never saw the world from the summit of Kilimanjaro. But he knew the mountain was special. You can see this too, even if you never go to Africa. Kilimanjaro is not merely a mountain to be climbed. It is a home for millions of people. It is a rich, natural landscape. It is a marvel that, if protected, can be enjoyed for thousands of years to come.

Africa stands proud beneath the mountain called Kilimanjaro.

It is much harder to catch a full breath of air on top of a mountain than it is at its base. Near Earth's surface, air molecules are pressed closely together. This air pressure forces air into the lungs. At high altitudes these molecules are spread farther apart. There is less air pressure. People breathe faster to get the same amount of oxygen normally available at sea level.

Kilimanjaro's summit is more than 3.6 miles (5.8 kilometers) above sea level. Unless you live in the mountains, air pressure up there is half of what you're used to. The lack of oxygen gives many people headaches. It cuts their appetite and makes it hard to sleep. In some cases, altitude sickness can become even more serious, causing swelling of the lungs or brain. Every year, a few people die on the mountain from these symptoms.

Kilimanjaro is dangerous because it seems like an easy climb. No mountain-climbing gear is required to reach the top. Children over the age of ten are permitted to go up. People have made the climb in wheelchairs and on mountain bikes.

Successful climbers take it slow. They pay attention when their guides advise rest, and they listen to warnings from their bodies. They remember that fitness and endurance may not be enough for success. They must also allow themselves time to adjust to the altitude.

Climbing the Western Breach

Kilimanjaro Quick Facts

Name: Kilimanjaro, the Mountain of Greatness; the summit, which is on Kibo, is called Uhuru, "Freedom Peak"

Location: Eastern Tanzania in Africa, on the border with Kenya

Distance from equator: 185 miles (300 kilometers) south

Origin: A series of volcanic eruptions beginning less than a million years ago

Major volcanic peaks: Shira (now a plateau), Mawenzi, Kibo

Elevation at summit: 19,341 feet (5,895 meters)

Elevation at base (Machame Gate): 5,942 feet (1,811 meters) [many sources say 5,380 ft/1,640 meters]

Number of remaining glaciers as of 2012: 16

Glacial ice lost since 1912: 82 percent

First Europeans to summit: **Hans Meyer and Ludwig Purtscheller on October 6, 1889**

Number of official trails: **7**

Number of trekkers per year: **About 35,000**

Difficulty of climb: **Ranked as "easy" compared to the world's highest peaks; no technical skill or equipment required**

Percentage of trekkers who reach summit: **Approximately 50%**

Local population: **1.5 million**

Ethnic groups: **Chagga, Maasai**

Official languages spoken locally: **Swahili, Chagga, English**

Major industries: **Agriculture and tourism**

Threats to Kilimanjaro: **Deforestation, erosion, fires, invasive species, overpopulation, poaching, climate change**

Mount Kilimanjaro overlooks the town of Moshi in Tanzania.

Chapter 1. The Mountain of Greatness

1. Johannes Rebmann, "Narrative of a Journey to Madjame, in Jagga." *Church Missionary Intelligencer*, 1849.

2. Ibid.

3. Ibid.

4. Ibid.

5. Audrey Salkeld, "Kilimanjaro: To the Roof of Africa." *National Geographic*, 2002, p. 39

6. Jane Barr and Arshia Chander, "Africa Without Ice and Snow." UNEP Global Environmental Alert Service, August 2012.

7. Salkeld.

8. Cameron M. Burns, *Kilimanjaro & East Africa: A Climbing and Trekking Guide*. (Seattle: The Mountaineers Books, 2006), p. 85.

Chapter 2. Life on Kilimanjaro

1. Central Intelligence Agency, "Tanzania." *CIA World Factbook*, 2012.

2. Jane Barr and Arshia Chander, "Africa Without Ice and Snow." UNEP Global Environmental Alert Service, August 2012.

3. Smithsonian National Museum of Natural History, "*Paranthropus boisei.*"

4. Globally Important Agricultural Heritage Systems (GIAHS), "Shimbwe Juu Kihamba Agro-forestry Heritage Site, Tanzania." U.N. Food and Agriculture Organization.

5. U.S. Geological Survey, "Mount Kilimanjaro, Tanzania." Earthshots: Satellite Images of Environmental Change.

6. Hans Meyer, *Across East African Glaciers: An Account of the First Ascent of Kilimanjaro* (London: George Philip & Son, 1891).

7. Barr and Chander.

8. Lonnie G. Thompson, et al., "Kilimanjaro Ice Core Records: Evidence of Holocene Climate Change in Tropical Africa." *Science*, October 18, 2002.

9. Tim Ward, "Setting the Record Straight on Climate Change on Kilimanjaro." *The Huffington Post*, June 20, 2012.

10. Lucky Severson, "Kilimanjaro Trees." *PBS: Religion & Ethics Newsweekly*, July 13, 2012.

Chapter 3. If You Could Climb Kilimanjaro

1. Henry Stedman, *Kilimanjaro: The Trekking Guide to Africa's Highest Mountain* (Hindhead, UK: Trailblazer Publications, 2010), pp. 262–279.

2. Audrey Salkeld, "Kilimanjaro: To the Roof of Africa." *National Geographic*, 2002, p. 233.

Chapter 4. On the Trail

1. John Rees-Evans, et al., "Threat of Accidents and Death on the Western Breach of Kilimanjaro." http://www.westernbreach.co.uk/accidents.html (accessed November 1, 2012).

2. Henry Stedman, *Kilimanjaro: The Trekking Guide to Africa's Highest Mountain* (Hindhead, UK: Trailblazer Publications, 2010), p. 133.

3. Audrey Salkeld, "Kilimanjaro: To the Roof of Africa." *National Geographic*, 2002, p. 152.

Books

Latham, Donna. *Mountains*. White River Junction, VT: Nomad Press, 2011.

Moss, Miriam (illustrations by Adrienne Kennaway). *This Is the Mountain*. London: Frances Lincoln Children's Books, 2010.

Pritchett, Bev. *Tanzania in Pictures*. Minneapolis, MN: Twenty-First Century Books, 2008.

Watson, Galadriel. *Mount Kilimanjaro*. New York: Weigl Publishers, 2009.

Works Consulted

Barr, Jane, and Arshia Chander. "Africa Without Ice and Snow." UNEP Global Environmental Alert Service, August 2012 (accessed October 27, 2012). http://www.unep.org/pdf/UNEP-GEAS_AUG_2012.pdf

Britain-Tanzania Society. "Meyer and Purtscheller Were Not Alone." *Tanzanian Affairs*, 1990 (accessed October 5, 2012). http://www.tzaffairs.org/1990/01/meyer-and-purtscheller-were-not-alone/

Burns, Cameron M. *Kilimanjaro & East Africa: A Climbing and Trekking Guide.* Seattle: The Mountaineers Books, 2006.

Central Intelligence Agency. "Tanzania." *CIA World Factbook*, 2012 (accessed October 23, 2012). https://www.cia.gov/library/publications/the-world-factbook/geos/tz.html

"Climb Kilimanjaro." *African Sun News*, February 16, 2013. http://www.africasunnews.com/kilimanjaro.html

Fosbrooke, H.A., and H. Sassoon. "Archaeological Remains on Kilimanjaro." *Tanganyika Notes and Records*, 1965 (accessed September 29, 2012). http://www.ntz.info/gen/b00770.html

Globally Important Agricultural Heritage Systems (GIAHS). "Shimbwe Juu Kihamba Agro-forestry Heritage Site, Tanzania." U.N. Food and Agriculture Organization, (accessed October 26, 2012). http://www.giahs.org/sites/httptypo3faoorgid31410/shimbwe-juu-kihamba-agro-forestry-heritage-site-tanzania/en/

Goldsmith, Edward. "The Traditional Irrigation System of the Chagga of Kilimanjaro." *The Social and Environmental Effects of Large Dams*. Cornwall, England: Wadebridge Ecological Center, 1984.

Harrington, Erin. "Panthera leo." Animal Diversity Web, 2004 (accessed March 8, 2013). http://animaldiversity.ummz.umich.edu/accounts/Panthera_leo/

Meyer, Hans. *Across East African Glaciers: An Account of the First Ascent of Kilimanjaro.* London: George Philip & Son, 1891.

Rebmann, Johannes. "Narrative of a Journey to Madjame, in Jagga." *Church Missionary Intelligencer*, 1849 (accessed through Google Books, September 17, 2012).

Rees-Evans, John, et al. "Threat of Accidents and Death on the Western Breach of Kilimanjaro." (accessed November 1, 2012). http://www.westernbreach.co.uk/accidents.html

Salkeld, Audrey. "Kilimanjaro: To the Roof of Africa." *National Geographic*, 2002.

Schmidt, Peter R., and S. Terry Childs. "Innovation and Industry During the Early Iron Age in East Africa." *The African Archaeological Review*, 1985 (accessed through Google Docs, September 30, 2012).

Severson, Lucky. "Kilimanjaro Trees." *PBS: Religion & Ethics Newsweekly*, July 13, 2012 (accessed October 14, 2012). http://www.pbs.org/wnet/religionandethics/episodes/july-13-2012/kilimanjaro-trees/11790/

Smithsonian National Museum of Natural History, (accessed October 17, 2012). http://humanorigins.si.edu/evidence/human-fossils/species/paranthropus-boisei

Stedman, Henry. *Kilimanjaro: The Trekking Guide to Africa's Highest Mountain.* Hindhead, UK: Trailblazer Publications, 2010.

Thompson, Lonnie G., et al. "Kilimanjaro Ice Core Records: Evidence of Holocene Climate Change in Tropical Africa." *Science*, October 18, 2002 (accessed October 2, 2012). http://bprc.osu.edu/Icecore/589.pdf

UNESCO. "Kilimanjaro National Park." World Heritage List, 2012 (accessed October 3, 2012). http://whc.unesco.org/en/list/403

U.S. Geological Survey. "Mount Kilimanjaro, Tanzania." Earthshots: Satellite Images of Environmental Change, November 4, 2012 (accessed November 4, 2012). http://earthshots.usgs.gov/earthshots/Mount-Kilimanjaro#ad-image-9

Ward, Tim. "Setting the Record Straight on Climate Change on Kilimanjaro." *The Huffington Post*, June 20, 2012 (accessed February 16, 2013). http://www.huffingtonpost.com/tim-ward/kilimanjaro-climate-change_b_1612864.html

WGBH. "Laetoli Footprints." *Evolution*, 2001 (accessed October 26, 2012). http://www.pbs.org/wgbh/evolution/library/07/1/l_071_03.html

World Conservation Monitoring Centre. "Kilimanjaro National Park, Tanzania." U.N. Environment Programme, May 2011 (accessed October 2, 2012). http://www.unep-wcmc.org/medialibrary/2011/06/28/f4e8dcf6/Kilimanjaro.pdf

On the Internet

Discovery Kids: Volcano Explorer
http://kids.discovery.com/games/build-play/volcano-explorer

IMAX: *Kilimanjaro: To the Roof of Africa*
http://www.veoh.com/watch/v17109043EhcysdAC

air pressure—The weight of Earth's atmosphere pressing down on everything on the planet's surface.

archaeologist—A scientist who studies human history and culture.

continental rock—The hard outer surface rock that forms continents.

crater—The bowl-shaped hole at the summit of a volcano.

cultivate—To prepare land for farming.

ecosystem—A group of plants and animals suited to live in a particular environment.

elevation—Height above sea level.

endurance—The ability to exercise for long periods of time.

erode—To break down over time.

evaporation—The process of changing from a liquid to a gas (vapor).

fossil—A hardened print or part of a living thing that died long ago.

glacier—A large mass of ice that flows over land.

hominids—A group of animals including humans and their ancient relatives.

irrigation—The process of leading water from a natural source to crops.

jinni—One of a class of spirits that can live on Earth and take human or animal form; the plural is *jinn*.

kihamba—A Chagga home garden.

lava—Liquid rock that erupts from below Earth's surface.

mantle—A layer that lies under Earth's hard surface, containing liquid rock.

missionary—A person who lives in other countries to teach about Christianity.

native—Naturally part of an area, rather than brought in from somewhere else.

passport—A booklet used for identification when traveling to other countries.

porter—A person who carries supplies up a mountain and works in campsites.

savanna—A grassland dotted with trees.

snowline—The elevation above which snow is always present.

sublimate—To change directly from a solid (such as ice) into a gas (such as water vapor) without passing through the liquid stage.

tropics—The warm, wet areas of Earth that lie just north and south of the equator.

About the
AUTHOR

Before becoming a freelance writer, Christine Petersen enjoyed diverse careers as a bat biologist and middle school science teacher. She has published more than 50 books for young people, covering diverse topics in science, social studies, and health. When she isn't writing, Petersen enjoys hiking, snowshoeing, and kayaking with her family. She is a member of the Society of Children's Book Writers and Illustrators.